Practical Record Keeping

Development and Resource Material
for Staff working with Pupils with
Special Educational Needs

Second Edition

Hazel Lawson

David Fulton Publishers
London

David Fulton Publishers Ltd
The Chiswick Centre, 414 Chiswick High Road, London W4 5TF
www.fultonpublishers.co.uk

First published in Great Britain in 1998 by David Fulton Publishers

Note: The rights of Hazel Lawson to be identified as the authors of this work
have been asserted by them in accordance with the Copyright, Designs and
Patents Act 1988.

David Fulton Publishers is a division of Granada Learning Limited, part of
Granada plc.

British Library Cataloguing in Publication Data
A catalogue record for this book is available from the British Library.

ISBN 1-85346-530-5

Typeset by Sheila Knight, London
Printed and bound in Great Britain

Contents

Acknowledgements

I should like to thank all those whose ideas, comments and enthusiasm have encouraged me and enabled the publication of the second edition of this book. Particular thanks are due to my colleagues at Greenside School, especially in the very final stages; to Joanne Hardwick for her most helpful comments; to Paul Smith for the cartoons; and to my long-suffering family, Keith, Dale and Niall.

Thanks must also go to the schools from where examples have been drawn:

- Breakspeare School, Hertfordshire LEA

- Greenside School, Hertfordshire LEA

- St John's School, GM, Bedfordshire

- Watling View School, Hertfordshire LEA

Introduction

The purpose of this book is to provide resource material for the development of practical record keeping for staff working with pupils with special educational needs. Particular reference is made to pupils with severe learning difficulties, though the activities are relevant to all areas of special educational needs including staff and pupils in mainstream schools. The activities are intended for all staff: teachers, learning support assistants, nursery nurses and teachers' assistants.

It is important for staff in schools to develop their own policies, systems, frameworks and formats for record keeping while bearing in mind legal considerations. The activities and examples in this book are designed to encourage staff collaboration. Many activities could contribute towards a whole-school policy on planning, assessment, recording and reporting. This policy will describe and define the systems within the overall aims of the school. Staff involvement in the development of this policy encourages shared ownership and commitment to the agreed principles and practices.

It is not intended that staff carry out all the activities. The activities are independent but often inter-related. Links between activities and follow-up activities are suggested. Activities are grouped in chapters to enable selection:

- Purposes, principles and practice
- Planning and setting learning targets
- Assessment and record keeping
- Developing and evaluating record-keeping formats
- Pupil involvement in record keeping
- Records of achievement
- Reporting.

Staff may wish initially to carry out some of the activities in Chapter 2, 'Purposes, Principles and Practice', in order to decide upon a focus for further activities.

Each activity is arranged in a similar way:

- Aims
- Preparation required
- Approximate time needed to carry out the activity (this may vary according to needs and interests)
- Instructions for the session leader and participants
- Discussion points the session leader may use for encouraging, developing or focusing discussion
- Follow-up: suggestions for further activities.

The activities can be carried out in after-school staff meetings or on staff development days. Often staff will be asked to split into small groups of three to six. Sometimes it is important for these groups to be composed of staff from different areas of the school. At other times class teams may be indicated.

Sessions can be planned and run by staff with little experience of in-service training, but it is important that the leader of the session is well prepared for the activity and is familiar with the instructions. Most activities involve discussion among staff and usually the whole staff are brought together at the end of the session to share and compare ideas. The management of discussion by the session leader will involve the need to question, explain, draw out arguments and points of view, clarify and summarise.

All activities undertaken should be evaluated both in terms of responses from staff at the time and by considering developments in record keeping which subsequently take place. Once developed, a record-keeping system is not static, but continues to evolve.

1 Current Issues in Record Keeping

Record keeping is part of a much broader process of which curriculum planning, assessment, record keeping and reporting are all integral parts. They are all parts of the teaching and learning process and have a complex relationship with each other. Record keeping is the written evidence of some form of assessment, for example, of pupils' learning or of the effectiveness of teaching. The management of record keeping continues to present an administrative and organisational challenge in schools.

The Education Reform Act (1988) formalised assessment and record keeping in all schools, giving schools a legal responsibility to provide information for parents. The Education (School Records) Regulations 1989 (Circular 17/89) require records to be kept on every pupil, including material on the pupil's academic achievements, other skills and abilities and progress in school. This material must be updated at least annually. Schools are advised to keep their recording systems simple but are required to present data on progress within the National Curriculum and provide supporting evidence. The *Code of Practice on the Identification and Assessment of Special Educational Needs* (DfE 1994) also requires that an assessment and recording system be in place such that information about a pupil's progress can be communicated to other professionals. Specific recommendations, as noted in the 1996 School Curriculum and Assessment Authority (SCAA) discussion paper no. 7, *Assessment, Recording and Accreditation of Achievement for Pupils with Learning Difficulties*, include:

- the use of a variety of assessment tools to identify need;

- the involvement of pupils in assessing and recording their own progress;

- the maintenance of sufficiently detailed and clear records;

- relating pupils' progress to achievement in the National Curriculum;

- the use of individual education plans and annual reviews as opportunities for formulating long-term aims and summative assessment;

- focusing at Key Stage 4 on educational and vocational skills, independence and social competence and pupils' skills in self-assessment.

This discussion paper followed research looking at the assessment, recording and accreditation of achievement for pupils with learning difficulties. The paper illustrates good practice and identifies criteria for evaluating good practice in schools in assessing, recording and accrediting the achievements of pupils making small steps of progress in the National Curriculum. This paper (SCAA 1996), the revised National Curriculum (DfE 1995), Code of Practice (DfE 1994) and the OFSTED framework (OFSTED 1995) all emphasise a broad orientation to assessment and record keeping.

1

Some current central issues include:

- distinguishing between achievement and experience;
- the recognition and identification of progress;
- target setting;
- the recognition of the importance of the process leading towards targets;
- the encouragement of the involvement of pupils in planning and evaluating their work and in records of achievement;
- a continuous rather than occasional basis for assessment and record keeping, integrated into the teaching and learning environment;
- the relationship between assessment, recording and the curriculum;
- the balance between individual and subject record keeping;
- the recognition of cross-curricular aspects of the curriculum;
- the relationship between formative, ongoing classroom record keeping and summative records such as reports to parents;
- recording in relationship to accreditation, particularly pertinent to Key Stage 4 and post-16 students;
- the wider public context of assessment procedures.

Many of these issues will be highlighted for discussion through the activities in this book.

2 Purposes, Principles and Practice

The activities included in this section are intended as introductory complementary activities and may be carried out in any order or as individual sessions.

The activities involve staff in discussion, debate and negotiation to identify:

- current record-keeping practice (Activity 2.1);
- purposes of record keeping (Activity 2.2);
- principles underpinning record keeping (Activity 2.3).

The outcomes of each activity can be compared. For example, current record-keeping practice can be matched with identified purposes or principles to identify gaps or areas of overlap. This may suggest areas for further development. Relevant activities may be located in other sections of this book, for example planning and setting learning targets, involvement of pupils, reporting.

Each activity in this section could contribute to the formation of a whole-school policy on planning, assessment, recording and reporting.

Activity 2.1 Current record-keeping practice

Aims

To identify and be more aware of the range of record keeping currently taking place as a starting point for further discussion or activities.

Preparation

Flip chart and pen.

Time

30 minutes.

Instructions

Staff brainstorm what forms of record keeping currently take place in school. 'Brainstorming' means all suggestions are recorded on the flip chart in full view without comment or evaluation.

Discussion of this list could then take a number of tacks:

- Compare different levels of record keeping and the amount of detail required. Is it public? private? personal to pupil? What format is it in: video, book, paper?

- Discuss advantages, disadvantages and the necessity of the different types of recording.

Discussion points

Remember to include the whole range of record keeping: for example, register, reading card, annual reviews, records of achievement, plans, video records, individual education plans, portfolios of pupils' work.

Follow-up

This activity can be linked with other activities in this section: Activity 2.2 'Purposes of record keeping' and Activity 2.3 'Principles underlying record keeping'. It also prepares well for Activity 4.1 'Linking the levels of record keeping'.

Activity 2.2 Purposes of record keeping

Aims

To identify and discuss the purposes of record keeping. Why record? Who do we keep records for?

Preparation

- Flip chart and pen.
- OHP transparency and projector or copies of 'Learning, teaching and reporting' sheet (p. 6).
- Three sheets of flip chart paper, previously labelled: Learning, Teaching, Reporting.
- Copies of 'List of purposes' (p. 7) (optional).

Time

40 minutes.

Instructions

There are three parts to this activity:

1. Brainstorm and record on a large piece of paper all suggestions for 'why do we record?' This may be carried out individually or in small groups initially, depending upon numbers in the group.

2. Show the transparency 'Learning, teaching and reporting' to make the distinction between record keeping for learning, for the pupils' needs; for teaching, to make teaching more effective; for reporting and accountability.

   An example is included in each case. Organise the brainstormed suggestions on the three labelled sheets of paper. This activity may in itself suggest further ideas for why record keeping takes place. One type of recording can cover a range of purposes so some suggestions may be included on more than one sheet.

3. (Optional) Finally, hand out the list of purposes of record keeping to compare with your own suggested purposes.

Discussion points

Why do we need to write down information?

The purposes may determine the level and frequency of record keeping. Record keeping is a way of bringing assessment information together for formative and summative purposes. No one assessment procedure or type of record keeping can meet all of these needs.

Follow-up

Match types of records currently kept (Activity 2.1) with purposes of record keeping to see areas which are well covered and to identify gaps in current record keeping.

For learning: to meet the pupils' needs, e.g. to acknowledge achievements, to increase motivation.

For teaching: to make teaching more effective, e.g. to demonstrate continuity, to evaluate teaching approach.

For reporting: to be accountable, meet legal requirements and provide information for others, e.g. annual report to parents.

Activity 2.2 Purposes of record keeping
List of purposes

For learning:

- to assess a starting point
- a record of what's gone before (experienced, encountered, covered, working on, studying, in progress, achieved, can do)
- to monitor progress, to record significant developmental events and learning steps
- to acknowledge achievements, increase motivation and self-esteem
- to help pupils with self-evaluation, self-assessment as an integral part of learning
- to help pupils to negotiate future targets, where to go next
- to help build up a record of achievement.

For teaching:

- to retain information: for transfer to summative documents, e.g. reports
  for transfer to another teacher
- to demonstrate progression, continuity and development for individual pupils and the curriculum
- to ensure breadth, balance and relevance between needs and the curriculum
- to plan for future aims, differentiation, continuity
- to evaluate teaching objectives and approaches
- to organise time, to assist in classroom management
- to provide ideas for future activities
- to share teaching approaches and ideas with others, collaboration.

For reporting:

- to parents
- to other teachers – continuity, team teaching
- to other professionals, e.g. social workers, occupational therapists, educational psychologists
- to head teacher, governors, LEA, DfEE
- legally: annual report to parents
  annual review for pupils with statements
  Code of Practice, individual education plan
  School Records Regulations.

General:

- for curriculum evaluation
- to provide evidence
- to enable organisation of teaching groups
- for accreditation.

Activity 2.3 Principles underlying record keeping

Aims

- To consider underlying principles of classroom record keeping.
- By consensus to agree principles of classroom record keeping.

Preparation

- Flip chart and pens.
- Paper and pens for participants.

Time

1 hour.

Instructions

Each participant writes down three statements to complete the sentence 'Classroom record keeping should not …' and three statements to complete the sentence 'Classroom record keeping should …'. This part of the activity should be carried out individually and without discussion.

Make a master list of 'Classroom record keeping should not …', taking one item at a time from each participant in rotation. At this stage there should be no editing or evaluation. All statements are recorded.

In a similar way make a master list of 'Classroom record keeping should …'.

From the second master list, 'Classroom record keeping should …', clarify all items. Discuss each item to make sure its meaning is understood. Items can now be withdrawn if they are covered by another statement. It may be helpful to letter the final set of items.

Evaluation now takes place. Each participant has five weighted votes, voting 5 for the item they most agree with, then 4, 3, 2 and 1. This should initially be carried out privately, then shared.

Add up all the votes to find those items most agreed with. General discussion of this agreed list of principles may take place.

Discussion points

The 'should not …' activity and master list serves as a comparison to the 'should …' statements. Evaluation and voting is not intended with the 'should not …' statements.

Emphasise the activity is about principles, what *should* happen, not necessarily what does happen.

Follow-up

Compare agreed principles with current practice. The final agreed set of statements can form part of the whole-school policy on planning, assessment, recording and reporting.

3 Planning and Setting Learning Targets

Planning in schools takes place on a number of levels. Staff may identify learning targets and plan programmes of activities or schemes of work for individuals, small groups of pupils, class groups, Key Stages and sometimes the whole school. Planning may be for an individual session, a series of sessions, daily, weekly, termly, yearly, for a Key Stage or longer.

The 1988 Education Reform Act and the introduction of the National Curriculum added an extra dimension to the planning process. Each pupil is entitled to receive a broad and balanced curriculum which is also relevant to his or her particular needs. It is important to consider the balance between providing learning opportunities through delivery of the curriculum and working on individual learning targets as identified in individual education plans. Specified curriculum content will suggest activities and individual learning targets will shape those activities to ensure relevance. Individual learning targets will also, at times, determine the selection of activities.

Thorough planning will give information about curriculum coverage, providing a useful curriculum record for monitoring issues of continuity and progression.

Activity 3.1 illustrates one approach to medium-term curriculum planning, brain-storming activities, identifying the broader subject implications and curriculum coverage of these, and planning a series of activities in more detail. Individual pupil learning targets would then be built into these plans. This planning should be shared by staff, and plans could form part of a resource bank for that topic or curriculum area. Activity 3.2 examines the setting of individual learning targets and matching activities with these.

Activity 3.1 Medium-term curriculum planning

Aims

To consider a collaborative method of curriculum planning.

Preparation

- Copies of topic web (p. 12).
- Copies of activity planning sheet (p. 13). A3 size may be more suitable.
- Copies of example (p. 14).

Time

1 hour.

Instructions

Divide into groups of four to six, working with staff who work with similar age ranges of pupils. Each group selects a topic. This could be from a rolling programme of topics used in your school; it could be subject-specific or cross-curricular. It could be for one class, one Key Stage or the whole school.

Planning is for a series of activities. This could be over half a term or a term or it could be for a focus week, with a whole week's activities planned around a theme.

On the topic web sheet, brainstorm possible activities for the topic. For the purpose of this activity limit brainstorming to approximately ten minutes. At this point do not consider activities in detail.

Using the activity plan sheet, plan six relevant activities for your chosen group. National Curriculum programmes of study, the school's schemes of work and pupils' needs should be considered in this planning process. Identify the subject implications of the activities on the sheet too. An example of a completed activity plan is provided as an illustration (p. 14).

As a whole group discuss this method of curriculum planning.

Discussion points

Brainstorming as part of the planning process allows for greater creativity than following a set programme of activities. Working collaboratively increases the range of ideas and encourages creativity.

The curriculum subject references will give information for groups about intended curriculum coverage. Subject coordinators could identify the implications for their own curriculum area.

Topic planning could be used to structure and monitor the curriculum over a longer term, for example a five-year rolling programme of topics for the school. The coverage of programmes of study could then be planned over time. Sets of activity plans can be kept as a resource bank.

Follow-up

The next stage would be to weave individual pupil learning targets into the activity plans to indicate the targets for each pupil within a session. In Activity 3.2 individual learning targets are matched with activities.

Activity 3.1 Medium-term curriculum planning
Topic web

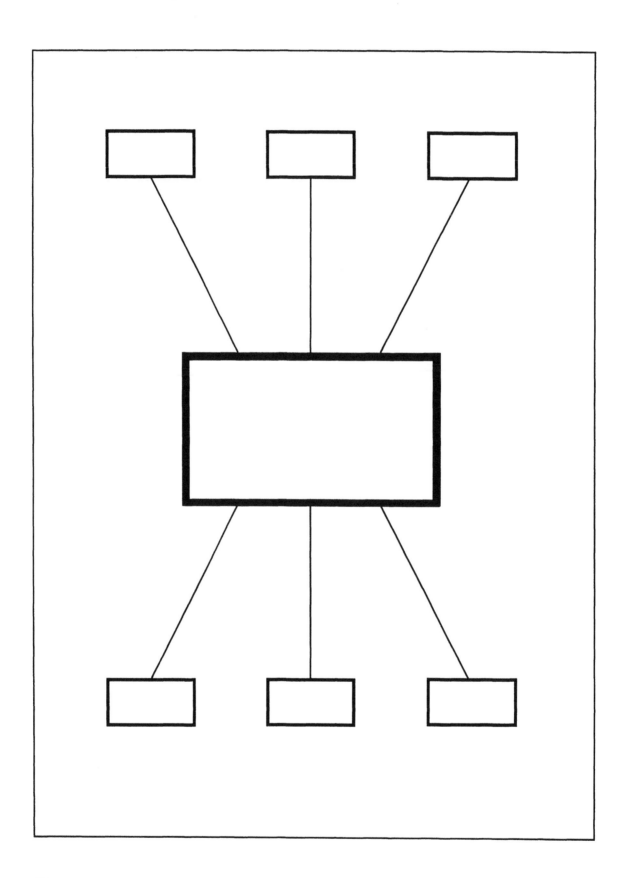

Activity 3.1 Medium-term curriculum planning
Activity planning sheet

Topic		Class/age range	
	Activities	**Curriculum coverage**	
1			
2			
3			
4			
5			
6			

Activity 3.1 Medium-term curriculum planning Example

Topic: Homes and Buildings Art/Design and Technology		Class/age range: P2 5–6 years
	Activities	**Curriculum coverage**
1	Introduction to topic on 'Homes and Buildings'. What are our houses made from? Look at walls in classroom. Explore some real bricks. Look at pattern of bricks and re-create. Discuss. Using clay, make some small bricks and build a small wall. Review all the 'made' walls and decide which is strongest.	**Design and Technology** Designing and making skills. Identify strengths and weaknesses.
2	Recap last week's session. Introduce idea of building/ making a pretend doll's house that looks like a real one, but is small. Look at a doll's house and discuss features. Produce large box for making doll's house. Task today: print walls to look like bricks. Recall pattern of bricks from last session. Prepare for painting. Mix brick colour. Print brick pattern on box. Evaluate together when finished.	**Art** Pattern and texture. Colour mixing. Printing. Experiment with visual elements.
3	Go outside to look at the school's roof to discuss what it is made from and what job it does. Inside, explore some real tiles, pantiles and slates. Discuss necessary properties, shape, size and how to fit together. Look at some pictures of houses and focus on roofs. Task today to paint the roof on our doll's house to make it look like tiles. Suggestions/ideas. Prepare for painting. Mix colours and paint or print. Evaluate when finished.	**Art** As above. Record experiences. **Design and Technology** Finishing techniques.
4	Look at pictures and discuss how inside walls are decorated. What does everyone have on walls at home? Explore some embossed wallpaper samples. Look for stripes and repeating patterns. Everyone makes their own wallpaper pattern for part of the doll's house. Choose colours and methods to paint or print. Review at end.	**Art** Explore pattern and create own idea. Choice of colours and techniques.
5	Look at everyone's designed wallpaper, now stuck on walls in doll's house. Comments. Look at house and suggest what is missing. Today, make windows which will open and close. Explore doors in classroom to identify 'hinges' and how they work. Make windows with simple hinges for doll's house using cocktail sticks slotted into straws. Evaluate whether they work.	**Design and Technology** Make joints which allow movement. Evaluate product.
6	Look at doll's house. Inspect all work accomplished. Identify what's missing. Furniture. Discuss what furniture is needed for each room and look at some doll's furniture. Decide what to make. Make pieces of furniture from either wood or clay with help. Review everyone's work, each person describing what they have made.	**Design and Technology** Shaping and assembling materials to achieve ideas.
7	Look at everyone's furniture. Decide which room is which in the doll's house and which furniture goes in each room. Each person puts in their own furniture. Look at finished result and make comments. Play with house. Introduce dolls.	**Art/Design and Technology** Interior design!

Activity 3.2 Matching activities with individual learning targets

Aims

To identify, then match, individual pupil learning targets and intentions of curriculum activities.

Preparation

- Paper and pens for participants.
- Staff may need copies of two pupils' individual education plans.
- Copies of activity sheet (p. 16). A3 would be a more suitable size.
- OHP transparency or copies of example (p. 17).

Time

1 hour.

Instructions

Working individually, list five main learning targets for two pupils in your class. Do this without considering curriculum areas. Think about the most important educational targets for each pupil. Staff may like to refer to pupils' individual education plans.

In class teams, where appropriate, or in small groups, discuss these to compare and to highlight similarities and differences in the emphasis of selected targets.

Individually or in class teams complete the first two columns of the activity sheet, listing activities for a typical week and noting the main aims of each session in curriculum terms.

Examine the potential for meeting your two pupils' learning targets within your weekly activities. The example of Tom is provided to indicate how this activity will be carried out.

Discussion points

How specific should targets be? Should they all be measurable? What effect does this have on the curriculum?

Consider the educational value and intentions of routine activities such as hello sessions, drinks time etc.

Pupil aims and targets should be identified through the annual review procedure and/ or agreed by staff, parents and the pupil where possible. How can pupils be involved in this target-setting process?

Follow-up

Consider all pupils in your class in a similar way.

Shadow a pupil for a week to examine whether learning targets are actually met within activities. Plan a group activity to take account of pupils' individual targets.

Activity 3.2 Matching activities with individual learning targets
Activity sheet

	Curriculum activity	Aims and intentions	Potential for meeting pupil learning targets
Monday am:			
pm:			
Tuesday am:			
pm:			
Wednesday am:			
pm:			
Thursday am:			
pm:			
Friday am:			
pm:			

Activity 3.2 Matching activities with individual learning targets
Example: Tom

Five main learning targets:

1. To make eye contact.

2. To use his right arm with control by purposefully reaching for an object.

3. To operate a block switch in the sensory room or with a tape recorder (cause and effect and control of environment).

4. To drink from a cup without a lid.

5. To point to photographs to make a choice between two options.

	Curriculum activity	Aims and intentions	Potential for meeting Tom's learning targets
Monday am:	'Hello' session	Group skills: turn taking, interaction, concentration. Use of vocalising, eye contact, signing.	1. eye contact
	Swimming	Physical skills. Movement. Fun, interaction with adult. Dressing, undressing.	2. right arm control through reaching
	Drinks	Use of vocalising, pointing, signing. Choice. Interaction with peers. Drinking and feeding skills.	4. drinking from cup 5. choose by pointing

4 Assessment and Record Keeping

Assessment is at the heart of the teaching and learning process, not a bolt-on activity. Assessment and record keeping involve the gathering of information or collection of evidence and the interpretation and judgement of it. Staff in schools are assessing much of the time. Often this will occur through informal observation and interaction with pupils, without being written down. More is thus assessed than recorded.

The range of assessment and record keeping needs picturing within an overall framework. There are different levels of assessment and record keeping: some are more formal than others; some are for groups, others are highly individualistic. In Activity 4.1 staff are involved in developing an overall picture linking the different levels of assessment and record keeping. Activity 4.2 concerns the identification of different practical ways of carrying out assessment in the classroom.

Activity 4.1 Linking the levels of record keeping

Aims

Through discussion and negotiation to develop a framework to link the different levels of planning, assessment, recording and reporting in a school.

Preparation

- For each small group of five to eight, a set of components cut up or made into cards.
- Large pieces of paper.
- Copies for each participant of the list of suggested components.

Time

45 minutes.

Instructions

Use some or all of the suggested components and add others of your own, if required.

In groups of five to eight, deal out the cards to each participant. Discuss and arrange the components (on a large piece of paper) into a 'diagram' which illustrates the process of planning, assessment, recording and reporting in your school. You need not use all components or you may add others of your own. Arrows may connect different parts of the process.

As a whole group share and compare diagrams. It may be possible to collate these and make one diagram which outlines the process in your school.

Discussion points

- Where do you enter the process?
- How long do elements of the process and the whole process take to complete?
- How frequently do elements take place?
- Where and how is the pupil involved?
- Consider the balance between subject and individual recording.
- How is assessment information used to inform curriculum planning?
- How is assessment information used to inform individual education plans?

Follow-up

This can be linked with activities 2.1, 2.2 and 2.3 on the current practice, purposes and principles of record keeping.

It may be useful for further development or evaluation of formats. Does each element of the process require a different format?

It may form part of a whole-school policy on planning, assessment, recording and reporting.

Activity 4.1 Linking the levels of record keeping
Suggested components

Accreditation

Annual report to parents

Annual review of statement

Assessment

Assessments from other professionals, e.g. speech and language therapists, physio-therapists, occupational therapists, educational psychologists, hearing and vision impairment advisers

Baseline assessment

End of Key Stage National Curriculum assessment tasks

End of Key Stage National Curriculum teacher assessment

Examples of work

Individual education plans (IEPs)

Keeping evidence

Learning objectives: curriculum

Learning objectives: individual

Learning opportunities

Long-term curriculum planning

Medium-term planning

National Record of Achievement (NRA) or Progress File

Observation

Pupil self-assessment

Recording curriculum coverage

Recording individual pupil experiences

Recording individual pupil progress and achievement

Recording significant individual pupil responses

Records of achievement

Reports

Short-term planning

Targets

Transition Plans

Activity 4.2 How is assessment carried out?

Aims

To discuss ways of carrying out assessments.

Preparation

- Either or both of 'Baseline assessment' or 'Assessment related to learning targets'.
- Copies of the activity sheet (p. 23).

Time

30 minutes for one task. 1 hour for both.

Instructions

Divide into small groups of three to five.

Baseline assessment

Imagine a new pupil starts at your school and records from a previous school or nursery have not yet arrived. Discuss *how* you would assess the two areas outlined on the activity sheet.

Assessment related to learning targets

Discuss how you would assess with regard to the given learning targets. They are not necessarily the same pupil's targets.

As a whole group compare and consider means of assessment and discuss which are the most appropriate.

Discussion points

- Consider the use of formal assessment schedules, setting structured tasks and informal observation.
- Are preferred means of assessment related to teaching styles?
- How can pupils be involved in assessment processes?
- How does the nature of the learning target affect the means of assessment?
- How can ways of assessing be built into the teaching and learning environment?
- What evidence is required? How does this relate to record keeping?

- When is assessment carried out? By whom?
- How can assessment information be used to inform curriculum planning?
- How can assessment information be used to inform future learning targets?
- Should assessment focus on the subject and/or the pupil?

Follow-up

Attempt to build assessment opportunities into curriculum planning. In Activity 4.1, assessment can be placed in the full system of planning, recording and reporting.

Activity 4.2 How is assessment carried out?
Activity sheet

Baseline assessment
How would you assess?

PHSE: social skills and relationships

English: writing skills

Assessment related to learning targets
How would you assess with regard to these targets?

Food Technology: to show awareness of safety in the kitchen

History: to make comparisons between past and present

Art: to understand that paintings can be representative of real life

5 Developing and Evaluating Record-Keeping Formats

The record-keeping format, as well as the level and style of record keeping, will depend on the purpose of record keeping, the style of teaching and the organisation of the classroom.

Activity 5.1 is concerned with the evaluation or the development of record-keeping formats. A number of practical record-keeping issues are highlighted for discussion and examples of possible formats are included.

Activity 5.1 Developing and evaluating record-keeping formats

Aims

To consider practical issues in the development, management or evaluation of record-keeping formats and systems.

Preparation

- Select, perhaps as suggested by earlier activities, either:

  'Evaluating a record-keeping format', an example of a format to evaluate (this may be an example from within your own school or one of the examples included at the end of this section)

  or 'Developing a record-keeping format', a type of record-keeping format you wish to develop, e.g. a medium-term planning sheet, an individual response sheet.

- Copies of the list of discussion points (p. 26) and the activity sheet (p. 27).

- Paper and pens for participants.

Time

30 minutes.

Instructions

In small groups discuss the questions and issues raised on the discussion points to help evaluate or develop a format. Complete the activity sheet if desired. As a whole group compare and share evaluations or developed draft formats.

Discussion points

Use the discussion points on p. 26 to highlight practical record-keeping issues.

Follow-up

Try out the format you evaluated or developed with several pupils or classes and discuss its future use.

Activity 5.1 Developing and evaluating record-keeping formats
Discussion points

Purpose

- What is the purpose of this record? For whom? The intended audience will affect length and style of records, e.g. use of jargon.
- Is the information really necessary?
- How much detail is needed? Would a tick or code be sufficient or are written comments important?

What is recorded

- What exactly is recorded? Is it progress? attainment? achievement? experience? significant events? coverage of curricular areas? work in a particular subject or core skill? work in relation to a specific target?
- Is process recorded? Is recording based on outcomes only?
- Is enough/too much information recorded? What level of detail is necessary?
- Is use made of information technology?
- Does it match the purpose of the record?

People involved

- Who records? Who owns? Who has access? Consider pupils, teachers, other staff, parents, head teachers, governors. The answers to these questions will affect the amount of detail and the style of the format, e.g. symbols or photography may be needed for pupil access.
- Is it easy for others to access or complete? Use of information technology may be necessary for access.

Timing of record keeping

- When is recording carried out? How often? How long does it take? Is this appropriate? Is it too demanding in terms of time? The frequency of record keeping will be partly defined by the purpose.
- Should record keeping only take place when there is something to record?
- Should record keeping be an integral part of the learning environment?

Storage and expendability

- Where is the record stored? How does this affect access? For how long is the record kept? These may again be determined by purpose and will affect the style of recording in terms of size, neatness, etc.

Personal preference

- Could you use this type of format? What changes would you make?

Activity 5.1 Developing and evaluating record-keeping formats
Activity sheet

Purpose
What is recorded
People involved
Timing and frequency
Storage and expendability
Personal preference

Activity 5.1 Developing and evaluating record-keeping formats
Example A

MEDIUM-TERM PLANNING FOR LOWER SCHOOL

SUBJECT: HISTORY	FOCUS/ASPECT: SPACE TRAVEL	KEY STAGE: 2	CLASS: 4	TERM/YEAR: SPRING 1998

LEARNING OBJECTIVES

1. To be able to recognise some planets within the solar system – earth, sun, moon
2. To indicate where 'space' is and to differentiate between space and earth
3. To recall and identify historical moments, i.e. man landing on the moon
4. To compare spacecraft and identify 'old' and 'new' craft
5. To role-play being an astronaut during 'galaxies' drama game
6. To respond to poetry, stories and video tapes with appropriate language/signing

ACTIVITIES

1. Looking at books and visual aids to identify planets, spacecraft and astronauts of different eras
2. Watching video footage of historical moments in space travel and relating it to time
3. Making/creating models of the planets and various spacecraft
4. Listening to poetry, songs and stories related to space travel
5. Role play – galaxies drama game

Presentation of Work:

Classroom display board incorporating planets, spacecraft and astronauts

Artefacts and visual aids

Oral assessment

Teaching Strategies:

Formal: Whole group
      Small group

Informal: Role play and drama

Resources

Books

Videos

Craft and display materials

Artefacts

Laminated posters

Assessment Opportunities:

Identify the sun, moon and earth on request

Identify 'old' and 'new' spacecraft

Recall historical information re space travel

Activity 5.1 Developing and evaluating record-keeping formats
Example B

Name of pupil _____   FLOW CHART FOR TAKING MESSAGES AROUND SCHOOL

NATIONAL CURRICULUM REFERENCES	KNOWING SELF	KNOWING OTHERS	GEOGRAPHY OF SCHOOL	COMMUNICATION	OTHER RELEVANT SKILLS	
E15 English sp & list L1 and Geography geog skills L1					Can give guided tour to a visitor around school	15
D14 & E14 English sp & list L1 Geography geog skills L1				Delivers a verbal message and returns with a verbal reply	Can ask for help if they get lost or cannot locate the person	14
D13 English sp & list L1 and Geography geog skills L1 E12 Geography geog skills L1 and PSHE				Delivers a message using an appropriately expanded sentence	Enters a room in a socially polite way	13
D12 English sp & list L1 and Geography geog skills L1				Delivers a verbal message using one or two key words		12
D11 Geography geog skills L1 and English sp & list L1				Delivers a verbal message		11
C10 & D10 Geography geog skills L1			Knows their way around school from any base	Delivers a written message and returns with a written reply		10
C9 and D9 Geography geog skills L1		Can find a person not in the classroom	Knows their way around school from a familiar base	Delivers a written message to a named person		9
C8 Geography geog skills L1 D8 English sp & list and Geog skills L1		Can recognise named staff or students from other classes	Finds a familiar room	Directs an adult around the school		8
C7 Geography geog skills L1 D7 English sp & list and Geog skills L1 + Ma AT3 3a level 1		Can recognise less familiar members of staff	Finds the school office	Using a symbol as a prompt takes a message to one other class		7
B6 English sp & list L1		Can find a specific person in the classroom				6
B5 English sp & list L1		Can recognise named members of the class				5
B4 & D4 English sp & list L1 C4 Geography geog skills L1		Can recognise named members of staff in class	Can find the hall	Listens attentively when spoken to		4
A3 and B3 English reading L1 C3 & E3 Geography geog skills L1 D3 English sp & list L1	Can recognise self in a photograph	Can find staff with a symbol or photo to help	Finds their own classroom	Understands commands such as 'give me'	Takes a message with a partner	3
A2 Science, life processes, L1 C2 Geography geog skills L1 D2 English, sp & list Level 1	Can recognise self in the mirror		Finds an area in the classroom	Makes eye contact when spoken to		2
D1 English Level 1 speaking and listening				Responds when spoken to		1
	A	B	C	D	E	

Starting at the bottom, and moving up and across, statements are cross-hatched to show pupil attainment   Breakspeare School

Activity 5.1 Developing and evaluating record-keeping formats
Example C

PUPIL RECORD		
Curriculum Area/~~Topic~~/Module Information Technology		
Pupil's name: Dale Chalkley		
Short term targets	– to control use of mouse buttons to load and manipulate word processing program – to learn close down procedures	

Date	Comments and Context	Staff Initials
3-10	Dale set up the Acorn 5000 and loaded the printer with assistance. He needed reminding to reduce the amount of clicking on the mouse.	FR
17-10	Dale set up and loaded 'Textease' independently. Practised close down.	FR
7-11	I changed the colour of my writing	FR
14-11	followed instructions to put different effects on the 'Textease' page. Clicking much reduced.	FR
28-11	Keith helped me to close it down. Dale finds it difficult to be precise enough when pointing the mouse for closing down.	FR.
3-12	Dale transferred his IT skills to English, demonstrating to the rest of the group how to load and use word-processing package	PA

Summary Dale has much reduced his mouse clicking to the necessary once or twice. He is now adept at setting up and loading 'Textease'
15-12-97 Fran Robinson

Future targets – to learn to close the computer down.
– to extend manipulation to further programs.

30

Activity 5.1 Developing and evaluating record-keeping formats
Example D

RECORD OF ACHIEVEMENT

PUPIL'S NAME: James Currie AGE: 13 YEAR GROUP: 7/8 (9)

DETAILS OF PIECE OF WORK: *(and date)* 4th Sept 97.
Creative writing - I invented an animal - told them all about it - gave them details and and asked them to do the same - give it a new name etc. Had previously read - 'How The Whale Became Stories - I had also read 'Dinosaur' stories - this seemed to sink in.

CONTEXT: *(e.g. set task, in small group, 1:1, staff support, own work)*
Set task - part of whole group. Staff on hand to assist with writing.

COMMENTS: *(from staff, pupil)*
Used stencils to create animal - Really thought about what he wanted him to be like.
Staff wrote this down - James copied - He enjoyed this. Worked well.

Helen Richardson

Breakspeare School

6 Pupil Involvement in Record Keeping

Greater pupil involvement in the teaching and learning environment is encouraged by the Code of Practice and OFSTED. One way of encouraging pupil involvement is through the processes of planning, assessment and record keeping. Under the Code of Practice (DfE 1994) young people must be involved in their own assessments and reviews.

Self-recording can be the recording of data or outcomes, e.g. recording pupil choices for drinks, or measuring and recording the growth of plants. There is an obvious overlap here with handling data in mathematics or science. Self-recording also involves more personal evaluation and reflection. The SCAA (1996) paper notes the following means of helping pupils to assess their own work:

- encouraging pupils to reflect upon their learning targets and what they have achieved;

- inviting pupils to attend the annual reviews of their statements of special educational needs and express their views;

- providing opportunities for individual pupils to review their progress regularly with a member of staff, using activities within personal, social and health education to encourage self-assessment;

- creating opportunities for all pupils to make choices and participate in self-assessment activities through the use of symbols, pictures, objects, signing and computers or other technological aids;

- using learning materials or schemes which include integrated self-assessment tasks;

- teaching pupils about the content and purpose of records and helping them to make choices about work, photographs or other evidence to include in their portfolios. Work at earlier stages will help pupils to use Records of Achievement effectively at Key Stage 4.

There are different levels of self-evaluation and recording:

- simple recall and concrete recording, e.g. a factual record of things we did;

- communicating preferences and choices, e.g. what I liked best and why?

- evaluating and analysing strength and weaknesses, e.g. what was difficult to do? What was I good at?

- target setting, e.g. what can I work on next?

Self-recording makes a valuable link between teaching and learning. It increases pupils' self-awareness and improves their self-esteem. Giving pupils some responsibility for monitoring their own progress may also in the long term reduce the time burden on teachers.

In Activity 6.1 staff can look at ways of involving pupils in recording. Through Activity 6.2 different self-recording formats for pupils can be evaluated.

Activity 6.1 Developing ways of involving pupils in recording

Aims

To consider ways of involving pupils in their own recording in a variety of activities.

Preparation

List of activities written on a large piece of paper:

- Changing a hamster: a science activity for three- to five-year-old pupils, some of whom have profound and multiple learning difficulties
- Number '2': a mathematical activity, five- to eight-year-old pupils
- Cooking beans on toast; a food technology activity, students aged 11–14
- Now Get Out of That fishing game: a technology and problem-solving activity, students aged 15–19
- Copies of activity plans for each participant (pp. 35–7).

Time

40 minutes.

Instructions

In pairs choose one activity from the list. Look at the relevant activity plan.

Discuss how you could involve pupils in recording during this session. Where appropriate devise a recording sheet. As a whole group share ideas for each activity.

Discussion points

- How can you involve pupils with profound and multiple learning difficulties?
- Does the age of the pupils make a difference?
- Does recording have to take place on a piece of paper? What alternatives are there? How can information technology be used?
- What can pupils gain?
- What are the resource implications?

Follow-up

Explore the opportunities for pupil self-recording in your own setting. Share and evaluate your ideas, formats and experiences with staff the following week.

Consider self-recording as part of a wider context of pupil involvement. Activity 7.2 considers strategies for actively involving pupils more generally.

Activity 6.1 Developing ways of involving pupils in recording Activity plans: Changing a hamster and Number 2

Activity Changing a hamster	**Group** 3–5-year-old pupils, some of whom have profound and multiple learning difficulties

Aims of activity
To be aware of what some animals eat and drink.
To have direct experience of an animal.

Resources
Hamster and cage with usual equipment inside, e.g. food and drink, wheel, bedding.
Clean sawdust and bedding, additional food.

Activity and teaching approaches	**Curriculum coverage**
Introduce hamster in cage. Watch its movements. Look at things in cage and discuss their purpose. Feel items as appropriate. Empty out cage and put in clean sawdust. Put in clean bedding. Put in food and drink.	**Knowledge and understanding of the world** Scientific experiences: experiences of animals; stimulation of senses.

Activity Number 2	**Group** 5–8-year-old pupils, some of whom have profound and multiple learning difficulties

Aims of activity
To develop concept of number 2.

Resources
Mirror.
Tray of pairs of mixed objects, e.g. 2 coins, 2 cars, 2 oranges.

Activity and teaching approaches	**Curriculum coverage**
Introduce self. 'This is me.' Use mirror to show 2 of self. 'Now there's two of me.' Pupils each do same. Talk about and identify body parts of which you have 2, e.g. eyes, ears, arms. From tray of mixed assortment of objects, pupils match 2 items, making sets of 2. Tell rhyme 'Two little dicky birds', reinforcing concept of 2.	**Mathematics** Exploration, handling and counting groups of different numbers. Use of number rhymes.

Activity 6.1 Developing ways of involving pupils in recording
Activity plan: Cooking beans on toast

Activity Cooking beans on toast	Group 11–14-year-old students

Aims of activity
To cook, with minimal supervision, a snack lunch of beans on toast.
To be aware of safety in the kitchen and in use of appliances (toaster and microwave).
To cook in pairs, helping each other and working together.

Resources
Kitchen equipment, including microwave and toaster.
Baked beans, margarine, bread.

Activity and teaching approaches	Curriculum coverage
Ask students to recall health and safety procedures for working in kitchen, e.g. hair tied back, hands washed, use of aprons, clearing up. Students recall and talk through how to use toaster, tin opener and microwave. Identify pairs and ask students to allocate tasks within each pair. Students then work together to make lunch. Eat lunch. Clear up, wash and wipe up. Evaluation.	**Design and Technology** Health and safety. Making. Use of appliances. Evaluation of process and product. **Cookery/Food Technology** Use of tin opener. Use of appliances. Spreading. Stirring. Serving. **PHSE** Work with a partner. Personal hygiene.

Activity 6.1 Developing ways of involving pupils in recording
Activity plan: Now Get Out of That fishing game

Activity	Now Get Out of That fishing game	Group	15–19-year-old students

Aims of activity

To work together to solve a problem as a team.

For all students to be involved in problem-solving activity.

Resources (Not all equipment will necessarily be used)

Different-sized bamboo canes.	Empty barrel.	PE bench.
Variety of different strength magnets.	Sticky tape.	Skipping ropes.
Steel cola can.	String.	Assorted stationery.

Activity and teaching approaches	Curriculum coverage
Set up equipment prior to lesson. Upright barrel with treasure (steel cola can) inside, with boundary line (skipping rope) about 2 metres away (i.e. out of reach of barrel). Introduce task to group, written and given as a challenge in a sealed envelope. Working together, group need to find a way of retrieving the treasure from the bottom of the deep blue sea (can from barrel). Establish some ground rules, e.g. not permitted to step over boundary, everyone to be included. Ask students to discuss ideas and plan for 10 minutes. Students attempt to carry out challenge. Review and evaluate activity.	**Design and Technology** Generate ideas. Design and make structures. Use equipment. Apply knowledge from science. Evaluate products. Work in teams. **PHSE** Work together as a team. **Science** Magnetism.

Activity 6.2 Evaluating self-recording formats

Aims

- To evaluate pupil self-recording formats.
- To consider criteria involved in this evaluation.

Preparation

- Copies of the self-recording examples A, B, C, D, E and F (pp. 40–44).
- Flip chart and pen.

Time

40 minutes.

Instructions

In small groups staff evaluate the six examples of pupil self-recording. They are not given detailed instructions or criteria, but asked to evaluate the examples.

As a whole group, they share and compare evaluations of each format. Notes may be recorded on the flip chart.

In small groups again, they consider what criteria were being used to make the evaluations.

Discussion points

Examples of criteria may include presentation, age appropriateness, purpose, relevant use of information technology.

Accessibility is a particularly important criterion. Is the pupil able to complete the sheet independently? Is an advocate, speaking for the pupil, required? Should there then be use of first- or third-person statements, e.g. 'I can ...' or 'Charlotte can ...'?

Follow-up

Apply these criteria to examples of formats in your own setting. Use these criteria to develop other pupil recording ideas and formats.

Activity 6.2 Evaluating self-recording formats
Example A

Leisure and Recreation Summary

Name ..Kirstyn............   Date ..13-12

This Term I have experienced:

Date:	Date:	Date:	Date:	Date: ....
swimming	climbing	sailing	bowling	ice-skating
walking	trampolining	canoeing	pot-holing	archery
basketball	cricket	tennis	golf	soccer
rugby	parachute games			

My favourite activity was/appeared to be:

Trampolling

Why?

Liked Jumping

I did not like:

Tennis

Why?

kept droping the ball

Next term I would like to:

bowling

Activity 6.2 Evaluating self-recording formats
Example B

Greenside School

Using the Microwave

Name .Anne....................	Date 19 November.......

1st course

Jacket Potatoes and Ham

2nd course

Ice cream.

I was good at

making my plate look pretty

I found it difficult Susan helped me
with the microwave.

The lunch was good

Target for next week use the microwave -

40

Activity 6.2 Evaluating self-recording formats
Example C

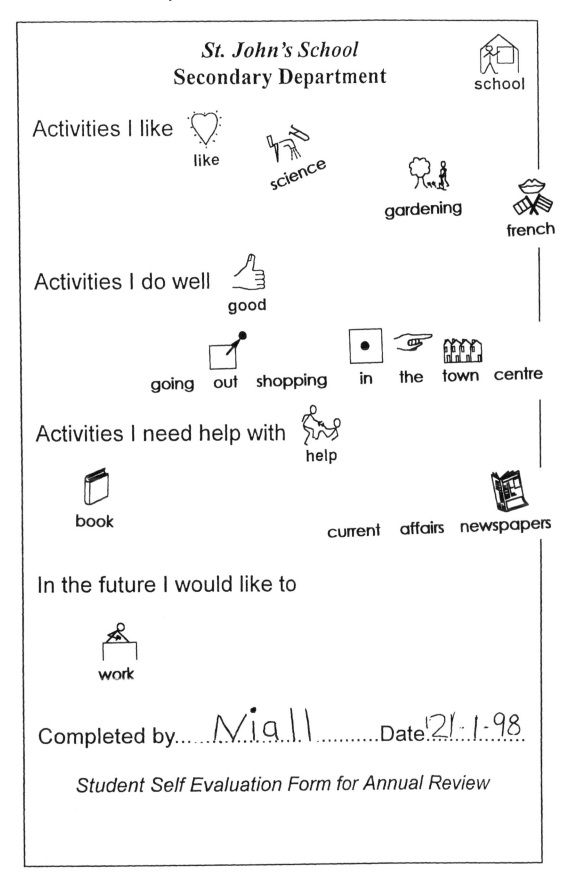

St. John's School
Secondary Department

school

Activities I like

like   science   gardening   french

Activities I do well

good

going out shopping   in   the   town   centre

Activities I need help with   help

book   current affairs newspapers

In the future I would like to

work

Completed by......Niall......Date 21-1-98

Student Self Evaluation Form for Annual Review

41

Activity 6.2 Evaluating self-recording formats
Example D

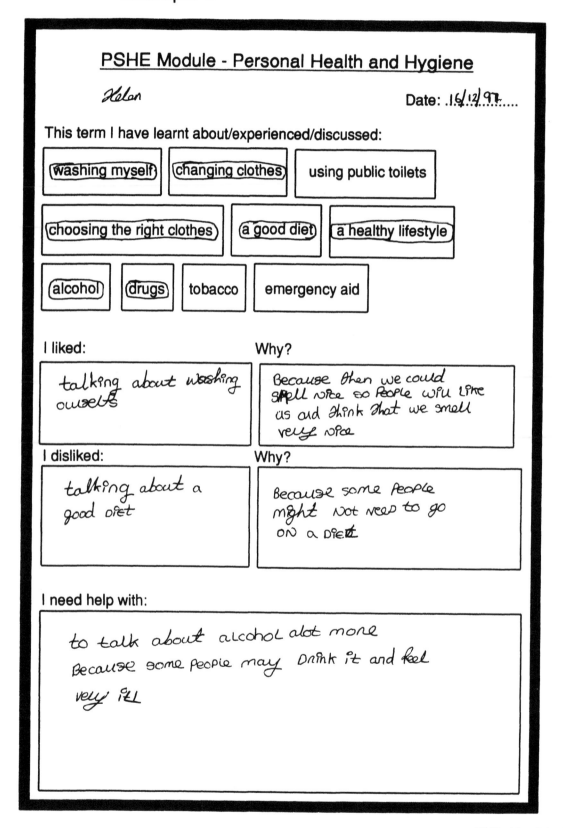

PSHE Module - Personal Health and Hygiene

Helen

Date: .16/12/97....

This term I have learnt about/experienced/discussed:

| washing myself | changing clothes | using public toilets |

| choosing the right clothes | a good diet | a healthy lifestyle |

| alcohol | drugs | tobacco | emergency aid |

I liked:

talking about washing ourselfs

Why?

Because then we could smell nice so People will like us and think that we smell very nice

I disliked:

talking about a good diet

Why?

Because some People might Not need to go on a Diet

I need help with:

to talk about alcohol alot more Because some people may Drink it and feel very ill

Activity 6.2 Evaluating self-recording formats
Example E

Breakspeare School   Name _____

Shopping
I can:

carry basket

push trolley

find items when asked

find items using shopping list

find my way around shop on my own

queue up

stack shopping at checkout

pay for shopping

pack shopping

Activity 6.2 Evaluating self-recording formats
Example F

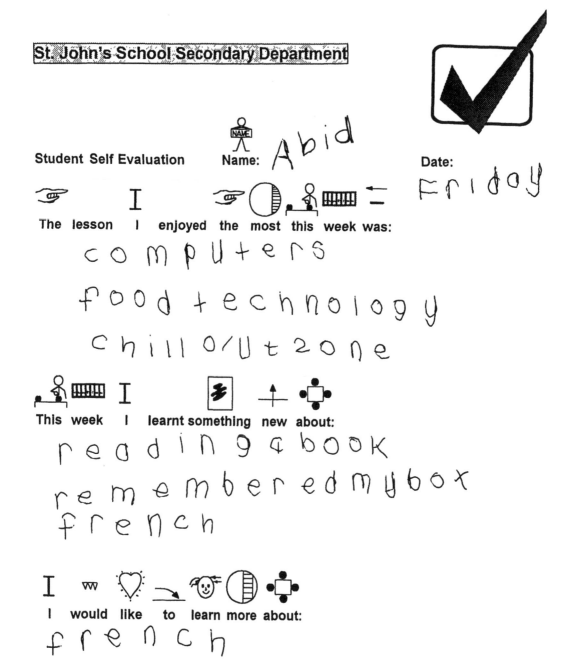

St. John's School Secondary Department

Student Self Evaluation   Name: Abid   Date: Friday

The lesson I enjoyed the most this week was:

computers
food technology
chill out zone

This week I learnt something new about:

reading a book
remembered my box
french

I would like to learn more about:
french

My behaviour this week has been:
good

7 Records of Achievement

Records of achievement, as a process, may bring together many of the principles and ideas examined in Chapter 2, providing a means of coordinating record keeping and reporting in schools. It is vital to stress that records of achievement are not just summative documents for presentation upon leaving school. The formative processes involved are crucial.

The National Record of Achievement (NRA), or Progress File, is presented to pupils at 16 or upon leaving school. Records of achievement are often, however, used across the whole age range in schools as a form of record keeping, to encourage pupil involvement and as a means of retaining evidence.

In Activity 7.1 staff are asked to consider the development of records of achievement across the school in relation to the key features of the records of achievement process. Activity 7.2 looks at means of involving pupils in a wider context.

Activity 7.1 Developing records of achievement across the school

Aims

To evaluate and/or develop record of achievement processes and documentation across the school.

Preparation

- OHP transparency or copies of 'Records of achievement: key features' sheet (p. 47).
- Copies of activity sheet 'Developing records of achievement across the school' (p. 48).
- Flip chart and pens.

Time

30 minutes.

Instructions

Read through the key features sheet together as a reminder of the wider processes of record of achievement.

Consider ongoing records of achievement for your school, either as a new development or in terms of evaluating current practice. In small groups, discuss and complete the activity sheet. There may be several answers as this is only an initial discussion phase.

As a whole group, compare and discuss your comments, using a flip chart if appropriate. Aim to agree on each of the headings and decide a way forward.

Discussion points

Can ideas be extended to all pupils, regardless of age and ability? Consider use of different media (video, audio, photography, use of symbols) for the summative document and for formative purposes. Are there implications for the curriculum, e.g. in areas of choice, assertiveness, decision making?

Follow-up

Through Activity 7.2, consider a wider context for pupil involvement. Activity 6.2 looks at pupil self-recording formats.

Activity 7.1 Developing records of achievement across the school
Key features

Pupil involvement

- Pupils are involved in the processes of recording achievement.
- There exist regular opportunities for pupils to review their own progress and plan the next steps.
- There is planned discussion between a pupil and a teacher.
- Pupils are involved in self-assessment.

Record keeping

- Record keeping is simple, flexible and manageable.
- Experiences and achievements are set in context.
- Positive achievements are recognised, acknowledged as they occur.

Reporting

- Reports are positive.
- Reports contain pupil statements and/or statements agreed by pupil and teacher.
- Reports acknowledge and give credit for the whole of a pupil's achievements and experiences.

Summative document

- Accessible to pupil.
- Owned by pupil.
- Includes personal statement by pupil.

Whole-school policy

- There is a whole-school policy on planning, assessment, recording and reporting.

Activity 7.1 Developing records of achievement across the school
Activity sheet

Format
Content
Selection Who selects? How? When? Editing?
Management Who is responsible? For what?
Storage
Pupil involvement Exactly how?

Activity 7.2 Pupil involvement

Aims

To consider strategies for meaningfully and actively involving all pupils in the wider record of achievement process.

Preparation

Paper and pens for participants.

Time

30 minutes.

Instructions

In small groups consider ways in which pupils are currently encouraged to be actively involved in the teaching and learning environment, including recording and evaluating, e.g. being consulted about their timetable, choosing within an activity, electing members of the student council.

Extend this to consider strategies for encouraging further involvement. Use the following headings:

- ethos of the school: the way pupils are valued, the atmosphere of the school

- recognising and recording achievement

- annual review procedure.

Share and compare as a whole group.

Discussion points

Consider:

- opportunities for choice, decision making and taking responsibility;

- use of information technology to encourage involvement, e.g. digital camera, concept keyboard;

- use of 'I can' or 'I like' statements. Is it acceptable to use the first person if a member of staff is interpreting for the pupil?

- communication, e.g. use of symbols and signing may facilitate pupil involvement;

- classroom talk, e.g. telling pupils what is happening and why, orally evaluating their work;

- parental involvement;
- involvement of all pupils, especially those who have complex or profound and multiple learning difficulties;
- age appropriateness;
- pupil control over the use of their time;
- use of advocates.

Follow-up

Pupil involvement in record keeping is one way of encouraging pupil involvement: see activities 6.1 and 6.2.

8 Reporting

The Education (Individual Pupils' Achievements) (Information) Regulations 1997 require an annual written report to parents on each pupil's progress. Schools are required to give comments on subjects and activities studied as part of the school curriculum, including the National Curriculum. Schools must also give a separate brief commentary to accompany the results of any National Curriculum statutory assessments. It is also mandatory to give details of a pupil's general progress, attendance record and the arrangements under which the report may be discussed with teachers at the school.

The SCAA paper (1996) states:

> Arrangements for assessment and recording in each school should allow staff to report accurately upon pupils' progress:
>
> - in all aspects of the curriculum, including the National Curriculum;
> - in reviewing statements of special educational needs or individual education plans;
> - at the end of each key stage;
> - at least annually, to parents;
> - to other professionals, such as careers officers and medical staff;
> - when the pupil transfers from one class or school to another;
> - on transfer to further education or employment.

One reason for record keeping is to collect information for summative purposes such as reporting to parents or carers. Reporting is not necessarily continued to the end of the process, but must be considered when planning and developing a record-keeping system. Written reporting is part of a much broader relationship with parents and carers. Much reporting takes place orally, with parents and staff exchanging information face to face.

The aim of Activity 8.1 is to encourage discussion about the nature and content of 'good reporting'. Activity 8.2 concerns the meeting with parents held annually as part of the annual review procedure.

Activity 8.1 'Good reporting should …'

Aims

To identify, as a group, principles of good reporting.

Preparation

- Make a set of 24 cards for each group of five to eight staff by copying the sheet of key features (p. 54) onto card and cutting. Four blank cards should also be made for each group, should participants wish to include features of their own.

- Copy the full list of features (p. 54) for each participant.

- Flip chart and pen.

Time

45 minutes.

Instructions

Give each group of five to eight staff a set of cards. Do not give out the complete list of features at this stage.

Deal out cards to each player in the group. Players take turns to select a card from their hand, choosing the phrase with which they agree most strongly to complete the sentence 'Good reporting should …'. Put these cards on the table until ten cards have been placed.

At this stage negotiation must take place within the group to add or remove cards. Only ten cards can remain on the table at any one time. Each group may develop their own means of negotiation.

Once all the cards have been used, this part of the exercise is complete. At this point there should be ten agreed phrases on the table for each group. If there is time, each group may then put their ten phrases in order of importance.

The full list of features should now be given out. Groups may now compare their agreed features by writing the initial letters of the features on a large piece of paper. It will be interesting to note areas of agreement or disagreement. Staff may wish to negotiate agreed key features as a whole group. This may be achieved by

- including those which appear in *all* the subgroup sets;

- including those which appear in a majority of the subgroups providing there is no strong disagreement. Phrases may be amended or reworded to facilitate consensus;

- examining the remaining phrases for overlap. Some may prove to be saying similar or related things. Such phrases may be combined, amalgamated or reworded to facilitate consensus;

- including more than ten phrases in the final set where consensus upon amalgamation or rewording is not achieved.

Discussion points

The emphasis is on principles rather than current practice. Some may seem unachievable, but if staff feel they are important as principles, ways of moving towards these principles can then be discussed and developed.

Staff could carry out this activity by brainstorming principles rather than using the prepared list of features.

Follow-up

- A workshop for parents could be held. They may wish to carry out the same activity.

- Staff may wish to compare and evaluate current reporting practices in the light of this ideal.

- A user-friendly booklet for parents (and pupils?) could be written to explain record keeping, reporting and the annual review system in the school.

Activity 8.1 'Good reporting should ...'
List of possible key features

A   involve pupils

B   involve parents

C   give parents the information they might reasonably want

D   include pupil, staff and parent comments

E   be jargon free

F   take place within the framework of a whole-school policy on planning, assessment, recording and reporting

G   include negative comments if necessary

H   include positive comments only

I   provide information about progress, achievements and experiences

J   identify strengths and weaknesses

K   suggest future priorities and targets

L   indicate what pupils have learned

M   summarise the pupil's performance

N   compare a pupil's performance with that of other pupils

O   place achievements in context

P   be built up from ongoing classroom records

Q   include a meeting between parents, pupil and school staff

R   follow a common school format

S   be word-processed

T   be concise enough to provide a format for the meeting with parents

U   be compiled from statement banks

V   evaluate the effectiveness of teaching as well as learning

W   be objective

X   detail progress against National Curriculum level descriptions

Activity 8.2 Meeting with parents

Aims

To consider positive and negative aspects of conducting meetings with parents.

Preparation

- Copies of the narrative 'Meeting with parents' (p. 56).
- Copies of the activity sheet (p. 57).

Time

30 minutes.

Instructions

Read the fictitious narrative 'Meeting with parents'.

In small groups, using the headings on the activity sheet if required, discuss and clarify positive and negative aspects of this meeting. Consider which apply to meetings with parents in your own school.

In a whole group share and compare.

Discussion points

Use the discussion headings on p. 57 to highlight issues.

Follow-up

Draw up an action plan for future development of meetings with parents in your school.

Activity 8.2 Meeting with parents
Narrative

Mr and Mrs Thomas are the parents of Sean Thomas, who attends Clover Special School for pupils with severe learning difficulties. They received a phone call from the school secretary one month ago to fix the date and time of Sean's annual review. They arrive at the school in good time and are shown to a couple of seats outside the staff room, which is to be used for the review meeting. A cup of tea or coffee is provided and all staff who pass them greet them warmly.

Ten minutes after the agreed time for the review, the head teacher, Mr Morris, appears and invites them into the staff room. He hands them one copy of Sean's review report which contains four pages of typewritten detail about his progress on his various programmes. Also present at the review are the physiotherapist, speech and language therapist, social worker, specialist teacher of pupils with visual impairment, class teacher and head of lower school. The head introduces everyone and proceeds to address the parents by their first names. They reply always referring to all professionals present by their titles and surnames. After ten minutes the social worker leaves, apologising, to go to another appointment.

Throughout the review the head chairs the discussion to keep everyone to the points, but sensitively tries to draw out Mr and Mrs Thomas's views and discourages the others present from presenting their predetermined priorities. Full records of ongoing programmes and short pieces of video of these are shared with the parents, and they are encouraged to ask questions and make comments.

After 45 minutes all areas of Sean's development have been fully explored, and the head asks the parents if they would like him to summarise the discussion. After doing so, he suggests the review report be amended in the light of the discussion and sent to the parents for final approval before being circulated to the others present. He then thanks everyone for attending. The class teacher invites Mr and Mrs Thomas to come to the classroom in order to see some work on display to which Sean had contributed some symbol labels completed on the 'Writing with Symbols' program on the computer.

Activity 8.2 Meeting with parents
Activity sheet

Discussion headings

Date parent receives report

Welcome

Pupil participation in meeting

Level of communication in meeting

Negotiation of pupil's priorities

Interruptions

Involvement of other agencies

Record of meeting

Seating arrangements

Timing of meeting

Positive aspects	**Negative aspects**

Bibliography

Black, P. (1996) 'Formative assessment and the improvement of learning', *British Journal of Special Education* **23**(2), 51–6.

Byers, R. and Rose, R. (1996) *Planning the Curriculum for Pupils with Special Educational Needs.* London: David Fulton Publishers.

Department for Education (1994) *Code of Practice on the Identification and Assessment of Special Educational Needs.* London: DfE.

Department for Education (1995) *The National Curriculum.* London: HMSO.

OFSTED (1995) *Guidance on the Inspection of Special Schools.* London: HMSO.

Ouvry, C. and Saunders, S. (1996) 'Pupils with profound and multiple learning difficulties', in Carpenter, B., Ashdown, R., Bovair, K. (eds) *Enabling Access: Effective Teaching and Learning for Pupils with Learning Difficulties.* London: David Fulton Publishers.

Porter, J. and Male, D. (1996) 'Using technology to record progress made by pupils with PMLD', *PMLD Link* **25**, 5–9.

Rose, R., Fergusson, A., Coles, C., Byers, R., Banes, D. (eds) (1994) *Implementing the Whole Curriculum for Pupils with Learning Difficulties.* London: David Fulton Publishers.

Rose, R., McNamara, S., O'Neil, J. (1996) 'Promoting the greater involvement of pupils with special needs in the management of their own assessment and learning processes', *British Journal of Special Education* **23**(4), 166–71.

Sebba, J., Byers, R., Rose, R. (1993) *Redefining the Whole Curriculum for Pupils with Learning Difficulties.* London: David Fulton Publishers.

School Curriculum and Assessment Authority (SCAA) (1996) *Discussion Papers: No. 7. Assessment, Recording and Accreditation of Achievement for Pupils with Learning Difficulties.* London: SCAA.

Walpole, P. (1996) 'The development of a curriculum record at Paddock School', *British Journal of Special Education* **23**(2), 62–4.

www.ingramcontent.com/pod-product-compliance
Ingram Content Group UK Ltd.
Pitfield, Milton Keynes, MK11 3LW, UK
UKHW050013280225
455677UK00025B/795

9 781853 465307